THE PLANET OF PUZZLES

DAVID GLOVER

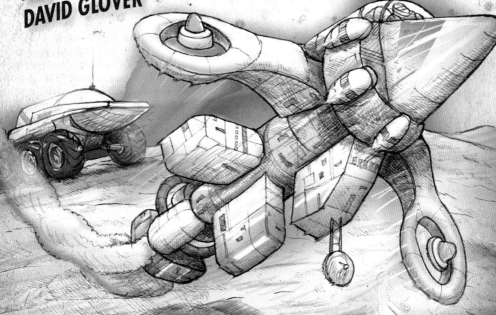

Illustrator: Tim Hutchinson
Editor: Lauren Taylor
Designer: Maria Bowers

Language consultant: Penny Glover

First published in the UK in 2011 by
QED Publishing
A Quarto Group company
226 City Road
London EC1V 2TT

www.qed-publishing.co.uk

A catalogue record for this book is available
from the British Library.

ISBN 978 1 84835 636 8

Printed in China

How to begin your quest

Are you ready for an amazing adventure – with twists and turns, exciting action and puzzles to solve? Then this is the book for you!

The Planet of Puzzles is no ordinary book – you don't read the pages in order, 1, 2, 3… Instead you must jump to and fro, forwards and back, as the plot unfolds. Sometimes you may lose your way, but the story will soon guide you back to where you need to be.

The story begins on page 4. Very soon you will have problems to solve and choices to make. The choices will look something like this:

If you think the correct answer is A, go to page 10

If you think the correct answer is B, go to page 18

Your task is to solve each problem and make the right choice. So, if you think the correct answer is A, you turn to page 10 and look for the   symbol. That's where you will find the next part of the story.

But what happens if you make the wrong choice? Don't worry! The text will explain where you went wrong and send you back to try again.

The problems in this quest are all about data handling. To solve them you must use your knowledge of tables, charts, graphs, averages and probability. To help you, there is a glossary of data handling words at the back of the book, starting on page 44. You will find all the ideas you need there.

As you follow the adventure you will be collecting the data you need to save Alpha Base. You will log the data on the electronic data pad you are carrying. Try to remember which data you have collected as you follow the quest. You will need all the data to complete the adventure successfully.

So – do you think you are ready? Turn the page and let your adventure begin.

Prepare for touch down! Your spaceship is about to land at Alpha Base on the Planet of Puzzles. You have been sent to replenish supplies and update their computer systems. But something is wrong. The lights are flickering. The airlocks are wide open. The computers have crashed. And the base crew have disappeared!

You have to rescue the crew! You must restore power, close the airlocks and reboot the computers. Then you can collect the data you need to discover what has happened!

If you are ready for the challenge, go to page 11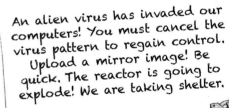

If you are still not sure, go to page 20

You step inside the Laboratory. It's chaos. Warning lights are flashing and the apparatus has gone berserk. Chemical flasks are boiling over and test tubes are smashing. The door to the nuclear reactor is swinging wildly. Computer monitors are filled with scrolling alien signs and symbols.

Then you spot a message scrawled on the whiteboard…

Go to page 20

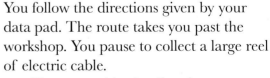

An alien virus has invaded our computers! You must cancel the virus pattern to regain control. Upload a mirror image! Be quick. The reactor is going to explode! We are taking shelter.

Vineeta

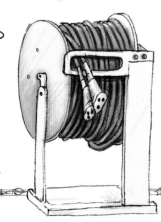

You follow the directions given by your data pad. The route takes you past the workshop. You pause to collect a large reel of electric cable.

You entered in the directions correctly! In just a few minutes you arrive at the solar cells.

Go to page 32

You type the commands to turn the undamaged satellite dish to point at Planet Z. Then you try to send a signal. Nothing happens.

A video feed shows the problem. The alien machine has escaped from the crater! It has cut out a huge chunk from the second dish! You must stop the alien machine before it eats any more!

Rhombus comes to the rescue! He bursts through the airlock, powers up his rocket pack and zooms to the satellite dish. There he faces the alien machine. It looks powerful and dangerous next to Rhombus. But a quick zap of electricity from Rhombus's power pack, and it's all over – the alien machine freezes like a statue.

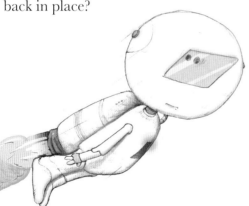

Now Rhombus must replace the damaged part. He sends a signal asking for instructions. How must he turn the piece to fit it back in place?

If you instruct Rhombus to turn the piece 90° clockwise, go to page 12 go to page 12

If you instruct Rhombus to turn the piece 90° anticlockwise, go to page 37 go to page 37

That's correct. The plants are growing in minutes – this should take weeks! The fruit is ripening in seconds – this should take days! Something weird is happening in the Biodome!

Go to page 31 Go to page 31

That's incorrect. Only aliens that have been eating iron and steel are attracted by the magnet. The magnet does not attract the aliens that have been eating aluminium and copper. Aluminium and copper are inside the metals set on the Venn diagram, but they are not in the set of magnetic materials. Aluminium and copper are non-magnetic metals.

Go to page 17

The control box shows the temperature. You can change the temperature with the up and down arrow keys. You decide to lower the temperature to minus 5°C. That should stop the worms!

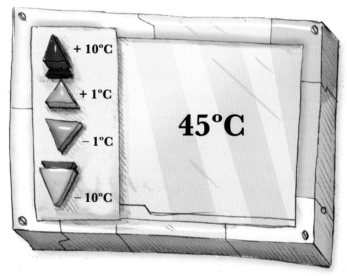

+ 10°C

+ 1°C

45°C

− 1°C

− 10°C

If you press the blue arrow 4 times, go to page 7

If you press the blue arrow 5 times, go to page 32

That's the correct number. You will need this number later to check that all the microbots are deactivated.

Now you must investigate the other parts of Alpha Base. There may be other problems to solve before you can locate the crew!

Go to page 14

You check 'Big'. Your data pad starts to get hot. Smoke comes from the keys! Messages flash on the screen!

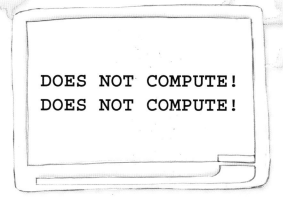

DOES NOT COMPUTE!
DOES NOT COMPUTE!

Quickly you deselect the box and try again. 'Big' is not correct. Look again at the chart. Some large items, such as windows, have not been damaged.

Go to page 28

 You approach the entrance to the Biodome. It's a giant greenhouse where Alpha Base crew grow food crops to be self-sufficient. As well as providing food, the green plants help to recycle air and water. A thermometer scale on the airlock door shows the temperature inside.

If you think the temperature in the Biodome is 4.5°C, go to page 34

If you think the temperature in the Biodome is 45°C, go to page 17

The temperature drops to +5°C. That's not cold enough! The worms are still wriggling! The spacecraft is still growing!

Pressing the −10°C button 4 times lowers the temperature by 40°C (45 − 40 = +5°C). How much more must you lower the temperature to make it −5°C?

Go to page 6

100°C

0°C

That's correct! The mode is the most frequent value in a set of data. Eight planets – that's the same as Earth's solar system!

Then you remember – the first space explorers discovered that inhabited planets have a similar size and temperature range to Earth!

Go to page 12

You step through the airlock into the Habitat and see the damage. It looks as if something has eaten the tables and chairs! You use a stylus to make a tally on your data pad.

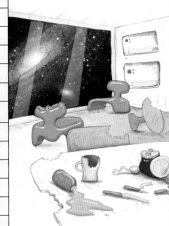

Frequency of Damage		
Damaged Items	Tally	Total
chairs	卌 I	6
tables	IIII	4
metal cups	卌 卌 I	11
plastic cups		0
metal spoons	卌 卌 IIII	**?**
plastic spoons		0
electric plugs	卌 III	8
knives	卌 卌 卌 卌 IIII	24
drinks cans	卌 IIII	9
computer screens		0
windows		0

You enter the totals in the total column.

If you enter the total number of damaged metal spoons as 14, go to page 23 ☆

If you enter the total number of damaged metal spoons as 12, go to page 38

That's correct! The safe door opens. You find the data stick inside. You plug it into your data pad to transfer the data it holds.

The normal way to write a date in digits is day/month/year. July is the seventh month of the year, so the 28th July 2254 is 28/07/2254. Now you can tackle the next part of the adventure!

Go to page 11

Outside the Habitat you see a small crater you had not spotted before. There seems to be a toy spacecraft in it. You use your data pad camera to examine it. It's not a toy at all! It's the ship in which the aliens arrived. There are lines of tiny alien machines marching from the spacecraft towards the Habitat dome! Then you spot strange alien symbols on the craft…

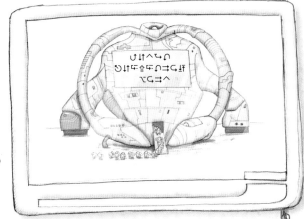

You program your data pad to translate the symbols. This is the translation table it displays…

↳	⇄	↳	↹	↕	↳	↳	⇇	⇉	↑↑	↓↓	∩	℧
A	**B**	**C**	**D**	**E**	**F**	**G**	**H**	**I**	**J**	**K**	**L**	**M**
↰	↶	↻	↺	↺	⌢	⌃	⌒	⌣	⌣	⇧	⇧	⇦
N	**O**	**P**	**Q**	**R**	**S**	**T**	**U**	**V**	**W**	**X**	**Y**	**Z**

The data pad translates the first word…

℧	↕	⌃	↳	∩
M	**E**	**T**	**A**	**L**

and the second word…

↺	↕	↳	⇧	↳	∩	⇉	↰	↳
R	**E**	**C**	**Y**	**C**	**L**	**I**	**N**	**G**

You use the table to translate the third word…

⌒	↰	⇉	⌃

If you think the third word is UNIT, go to page 13

If you think the third word is SHIP, go to page 36 ☆

Rhombus puts his robot hands over his robot eyes and shakes his robot head!

Check the chart again. Planet X hardly has any oxygen in its atmosphere. How much oxygen does Planet Z have in its atmosphere?

Go to page 16

You program your data pad to analyse the Biodome soil. You are amazed when you compare its bar chart to normal soil.

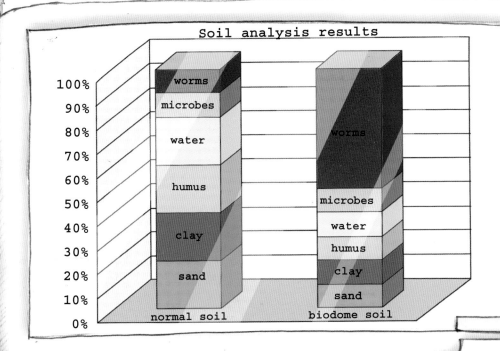

Soil analysis results

normal soil (bottom to top): sand, clay, humus, water, microbes, worms

biodome soil (bottom to top): sand, clay, humus, water, microbes, worms

Scale: 0% to 100%

If you think the Biodome soil has more worms than normal soil, go to page 43

If you think the Biodome soil has fewer worms than normal soil, go to page 40

That's correct! The aliens eating the steel are attracted to the magnet. The aliens eating aluminium and copper aren't. These metals aren't magnetic.

Go to page 40

Back at your spaceship you refill your oxygen tanks and grab a high energy food ration. You decide you should take a closer look at the alien craft. The more data you have about the alien threat the better.

Go to page 21

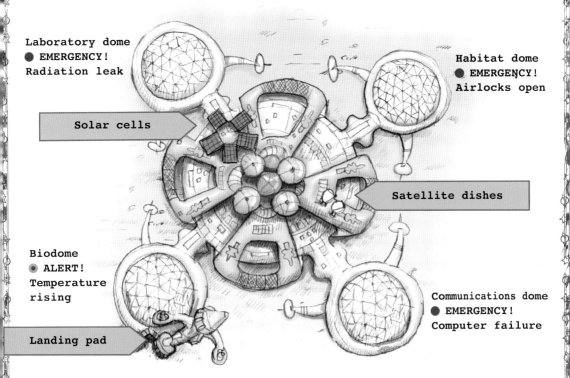

Your spaceship touches down on the landing pad. The map on your computer screen shows the base layout.

Laboratory dome
● EMERGENCY!
Radiation leak

Solar cells

Habitat dome
● EMERGENCY!
Airlocks open

Satellite dishes

Biodome
● ALERT!
Temperature
rising

Communications dome
● EMERGENCY!
Computer failure

Landing pad

Red emergency lights flash next to the Habitat, Laboratory and Communications domes. An amber warning light shows that the temperature is rising in the Biodome! You pull on your spacesuit.

Go to page 14

You've entered the wrong code! The warning lights start to flash. You have one more attempt before the safe locks you out.

August is the eighth month of the year. Which number month is July?

Go to page 22

You ask the computer to search for planets about the same size as Earth in the four 8-planet star systems. But there is one in each! To help decide which may be inhabited you ask for the maximum and minimum temperatures to be shown as well.

Planet	Minimum temperature °C	Maximum temperature °C
Earth	−90	60
Planet W star system 3	−90	200
Planet X star system 5	−95	55
Planet Y star system 8	−150	60
Planet Z star system 10	−85	65

If you think that planets W and Y have the same temperature range as Earth, go to page 22

If you think that planets X and Z have the same temperature range as Earth, go to page 16

You try to connect to the Laboratory computers through your data pad. A warning appears...

　　To get inside and stop the attack, you must key the entry code into the airlock touch pad.

Go to page 37

VIRUS ATTACK!

ALL COMPUTER DATA JUMBLED!

LABORATORY SAFETY SYSTEMS FAILING!

RADIATION LEAK!

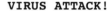

That's the correct instruction! Rhombus turns the piece. It fits back perfectly. The dish begins to transmit your message.

Go to page 19

You approach the Communications dome airlock. You plan to contact the aliens responsible for the damage to Alpha Base. Before trying to enter, you make a checklist of the information you will need. You click the check boxes next to each piece of data you have collected.

☐ Data from base security data stick
☐ Number of metal recycling machines
☐ Contact telephone number on Planet Zorgon
☐ Serial number of recycling worms

If you can click all four boxes, go to page 38

If you cannot click all the boxes, you must find the missing data, go to page 14

'METAL RECYCLING UNIT'; that doesn't sound like an alien warship! But it's out of control. Its metal-munching machines will destroy the Habitat dome if your electricity connection fails.

You collect a plastic storage bin from your spaceship. Carefully you lift the unit from the crater. You seal it inside the bin. That should stop any more tiny machines from invading the base!

As you go back into the Habitat dome the two suns rise over the horizon. The first rays of sunlight strike the solar cells. A ripple of electricity flows over all the metal surfaces in the dome.

You examine the surfaces with your microscope. The alien machines have all stopped working. They are dropping to the floor like dead flies! Your plan has worked!

Go to page 22

That's correct! When it has taken in all the living things in the Biodome, the unit will stop growing.

Go to page 43 ☆

13

Which part of Alpha Base should you investigate next?

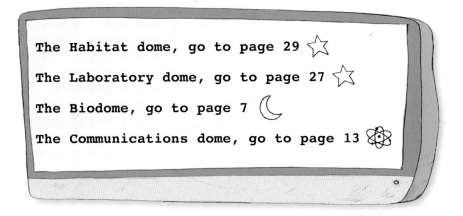

The Habitat dome, go to page 29 ☆

The Laboratory dome, go to page 27 ☆

The Biodome, go to page 7 ☾

The Communications dome, go to page 13 ⚛

Now you have the water and soil data you think of a theory to explain what is happening. You organize your ideas in a flow chart on your data pad...

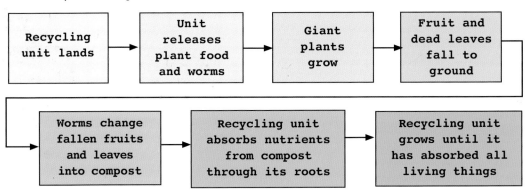

| Recycling unit lands | → | Unit releases plant food and worms | → | Giant plants grow | → | Fruit and dead leaves fall to ground |

| Worms change fallen fruits and leaves into compost | → | Recycling unit absorbs nutrients from compost through its roots | → | Recycling unit grows until it has absorbed all living things |

If you predict that the recycling unit will grow forever, go to page 15

If you predict that the recycling unit will eventually stop growing, go to page 13

If you predict that the recycling unit will grow forever, go to page 15

If you predict that the recycling unit will eventually stop growing, go to page 13

You chose the more likely combination! Three of the four combinations have at least one green. Only one has two reds.

The inner door of the airlock slides open. You enter the Laboratory.

Go to page 4

That's correct! The height of the columns shows the number of damaged knives is 24; the number of damaged spoons is 14. The difference between 24 and 14 is 10.

Go to page 28

No, the recycling unit cannot grow forever. Eventually all the materials from the living things in the Biodome will be absorbed into its body. Look at the prediction in the final box of the flow chart.

Go to page 14

A countdown clock appears on a computer monitor. In 60 seconds the reactor will explode! 60, 59, 58... You must act fast! You use the risk prediction app on your data pad to help decide what to do. These are the results it produces:

Possible actions	Probability of explosion
Do nothing	1.0
Cut reactor power supply	0.5
Restart reactor computer	0.1
Turn on reactor cooling fans	0.4

There is time for only one action. You make a decision.

If you cut the reactor power supply, go to page 38 ☆

If you restart the reactor computer, go to page 42

That's correct! Planets X and Z seem to be most similar to Earth. Could one of them be Zorgon? All known intelligent life forms breathe oxygen. You ask the computer to compare the gases in the two planets' atmospheres to the gases in Earth's atmosphere.

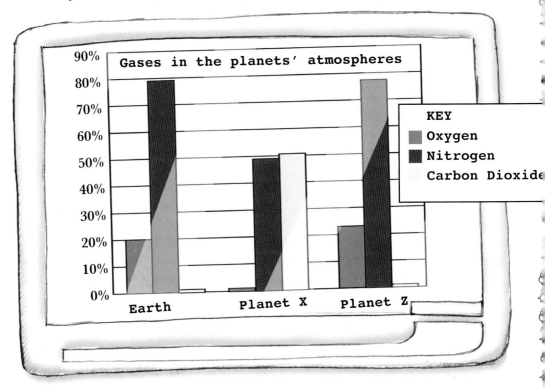

Gases in the planets' atmospheres

KEY
Oxygen
Nitrogen
Carbon Dioxide

Earth   Planet X   Planet Z

If you think Planet X has a similar atmosphere to Earth, go to page 10

If you think Planet Z has a similar atmosphere to Earth, go to page 28

That's correct! All the damaged items are made from metal. Something in Alpha Base seems to be 'eating' metal! All the knives are metal and they are all eaten, but some spoons are plastic, so they have not been attacked.

You must act quickly before all the metal parts of Alpha Base are destroyed!

Go to page 26

You try to think of a way to stop the alien machines. There's no air left in the Habitat, so you can't use a vacuum cleaner to suck them up. But then you have an idea – the aliens are made from metal. Some metals are attracted by magnets! You search the data pad for more information about magnets and metals. You find this chart. It's a Venn diagram.

Magnetic materials

Metals

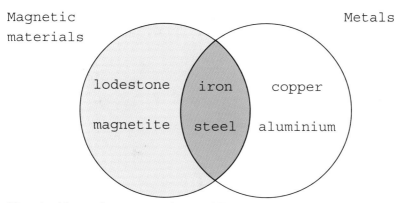

lodestone

iron

copper

magnetite

steel

aluminium

You decide to do an experiment. Your spacesuit has magnetic boots to hold you in place in outer space. You unscrew one of the magnets from the sole of your boot. You brush the magnet over different objects. Then you look at the magnet and the objects with the microscope.

If you think all the aliens will be magnetic, go to page 6

If you think only some of the aliens will be magnetic, go to page 10

You think the temperature inside is 45°C. That's hotter than it should be. You turn on the cooling system in your spacesuit and pass through the airlock.

You were right. It's like a rainforest in here. The plants are growing out of control. The carrots are as tall as trees. The sunflowers are as big as cartwheels. The tomatoes are like footballs!

Go to page 39

You follow the directions given by the data pad. The route seems to be taking you behind Alpha Base. This doesn't seem right!

Then, among the craters, you see movement. It's one of the alien machines. But this is not like the tiny ones in the Habitat. It's nearly eaten all of one of the satellite radio dishes! It's huge! The alien's mechanical head swivels. The electronic eyes spot you. It starts to lumber towards you on its mechanical legs. Its robot arms end in giant pliers. They can tear metal like paper!

Suddenly there is a flash from behind you. It's a powerful laser beam. A smoking crater appears in front of the alien. It trips and falls in. It cannot climb out! Who or what came to your rescue?

The numbers of the grid squares are coordinates. You started in square 9, 7. If you look along the numbers at the bottom of the grid you see that 9 is the column for your square. If you look up the side, you will see that 7 is the number for your row.

When you enter coordinates you always put the horizontal one first (the number along the bottom) and the vertical one second (the number up the side).

Go to page 35

Go to page 35

That's correct! Someone has added 25% alien plant food to the water!

Go to page 10

Then you see something strange at the centre of the Biodome. It's a spacecraft. But it has roots and leaves! It's growing! There is something printed on the side of the craft. Your data pad translates the alien text to 'BIODEGRADABLES RECYCLING UNIT'.

Go to page 14

Your signal is answered. A voice replies in a language that sounds like a bird singing! But the computer translates it automatically.

"Thank you for calling Planet Zorgon Interplanetary telephone exchange. How can I help?"

"I need to speak with someone at Galactic Recycling Ltd."

"Do you have a number?" the operator asks.

You give the number from the data gathering unit. "Zorgon 112 345 2011 please."

"Putting you through," says the operator.

Go to page 31

"Your call is in a queue," says the automated voice. "Your call will be answered shortly. We value your custom."

But then you are through. It's a video link! A strange but friendly looking alien appears on the screen.

"Good afternoon. You are speaking to Zapie. Can I take your account number please?"

You explain that you do not have an account number. You had never heard of Planet Zorgon or Galactic Recycling until their spacecraft started destroying Alpha Base. Zapie is horrified. He cannot apologize enough. A faulty batch of recycling units has been flying to distant planets at random. They should only land on abandoned planets to recover materials and data which are no longer needed! Yours is the 27th complaint today!

Go to page 23

You enter 'alien virus' in the search program on your data pad. After a few moments this is what the screen displays.

Common alien viruses

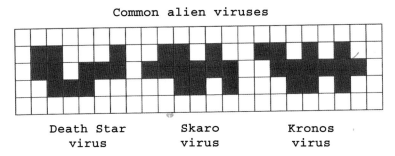

Death Star   Skaro   Kronos
   virus   virus   virus

You look at the computer screens. You see the virus patterns in the alien text. The patterns are mirror images of one of the patterns on your data pad!

If you identify the virus as the Skaro virus, go to page 36

If you identify the virus as the Kronos virus, go to page 37

 Don't be afraid. It's a challenging adventure, but help is nearby. When you are stuck or in danger, a mysterious helper will guide you and keep you safe. Just follow the instructions one at a time, and see how far you get. You may be surprised by how much you know! Good luck.

Go to page 11

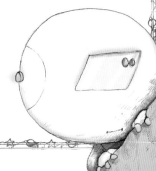

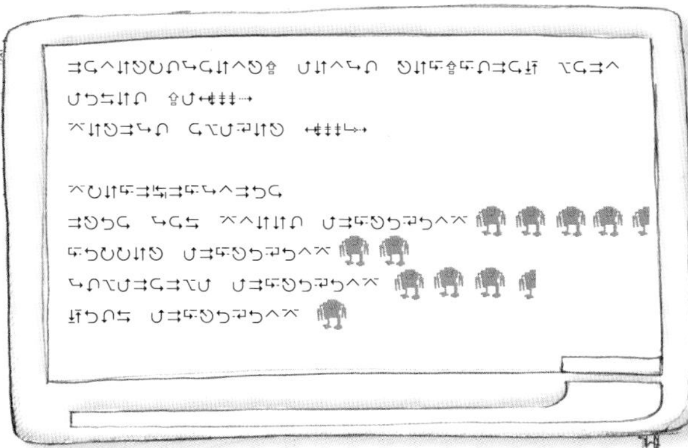

With the alien ship still in the plastic bin, you set up a wireless connection to the ship with your data pad. Data download onto your data pad screen...

It looks like gibberish. Then you start the translation program...

```
ㅋㅇ∧∏Ꙋ∪�∩Ꙍ⅃∏∧Ꙋ⚡ ∪∏∧⅃∩ Ꙋ∏ꟻꙜꟻ�∏ꙋ⅃ꟻ ⅄ꅂꙌ∧
∪Ꙍ⅃∏Ꙋ ⚡∪ᛙ++ᛙ⤙
✕∏Ꙍꙋ⅃∩ ꅂ⅄∪ꟼ∏Ꙋ ᛙᛙᛙ⤙
```
```
✕∪∏ꟻꙌꙋꟻ⅄∧ꙌꙌꙌ
ꙋꙌꙌꙌ ꙋꅂꙌ ✕∧∏∏∩ ∪ꟻꟼꙊꙌꟻꙌ∧✕ 🤖🤖🤖
ꟻꙊ∪∪∏Ꙋ ∪ꟻꟼꙊꙌꟻꙌ∧✕ 🤖🤖
ꙋ∩⅄∪ꟻꙋꟻ⅄∪ ∪ꟻꟼꙊꙌꟻꙌ∧✕ 🤖🤖🤖
∏ꟻꙌꙌ ∪ꟻꟼꙊꙌꟻꙌ∧✕ 🤖
```

```
INTERPLANETRY METAL RECYCLING UNIT
MODEL: XM10004
SERIAL: NUMBER 100094

SPECIFICATION:

IRON AND STEEL MICROBOTS

COPPER MICROBOTS

ALUMINIUM MICROBOTS

GOLD MICROBOTS
```

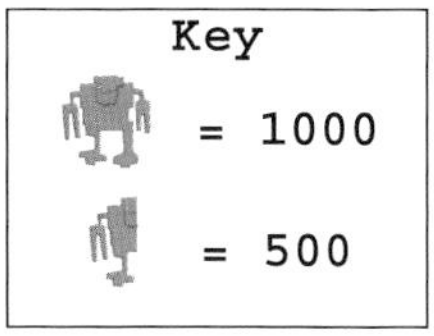

Key		
🤖	=	1000
🤖	=	500

```
MODE OF OPERATION: MICROBOTS GATHER ALL METALS WITHIN
50 KM OF LANDING POINT. MICROBOTS TRANSFORM INTO
SPACECRAFT WHEN GROWTH COMPLETE. SPACECRAFT FLY BACK
TO OWNER AUTOMATICALLY.

WARNING: FOR USE ON ABANDONED PLANETS ONLY. IT IS
STRICTLY AGAINST INTERPLANETARY LAW TO ACTIVATE THIS
UNIT ON INHABITED PLANETS!

ALSO AVAILABLE IN THIS SERIES:
MODEL XB10004 BIODEGRADABLE RECYCLING
MODEL XD10004 DATA GATHERING

MANUFACTURED BY: GALACTIC RECYCLING LTD, UNIT 3A,
INDUSTRY PARK, PLANET ZORGON
```

It's a user manual! The recycling unit has reached Alpha Base by accident. You copy the serial number. You see that the user manual uses pictograms to give the numbers of microbots. You decide to work out the total number, and enter it into your data pad.

If the number you enter is 1100, go to page 33

If the number you enter is 11,000, go to page 6

You point to the images of planets W and Y on the computer screen. Rhombus's eyes start to flash. Smoke comes from his battery pack. They are the wrong planets!

The range is the difference between the lowest and the highest value. Earth's maximum temperature is 60°C and its minimum is –90°C. This means that the range is 150 degrees. Which two planets have the same temperature ranges?

Quickly, check again before Rhombus bursts into flames!

Go to page 12

You have stopped the alien machines in the Habitat. Now you must explore the other parts of Alpha Base to rescue the crew. Then you remember Amy's message. You must find the data stick! Without it you will not be able to enter the secure parts of the base!

Amy said they had put it somewhere safe. Of course – the Habitat safe box! You spot the safe box on the wall. It's made from super strength diamond layers to resist any attack. It's not metal, so the aliens haven't damaged it. You look up Amy's details on your data pad...

```
Amy: Station
   Commander
Date of birth:
28th July 2254
```

The key pad on the safe has only numbers and a slash sign. So you guess you must enter the date in number form.

If you enter 28/07/2254, go to page 8 ☆

If you enter 28/08/2254, go to page 11

That's correct. There are 14 damaged metal spoons.

A tally is a quick way to count the numbers of different things or events. The table of the numbers is a frequency table. In this frequency table each tally mark stands for 1.

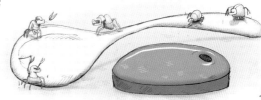

Go to page 30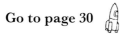

Your data pad makes the call. Vineeta's data pad answers. First you see the inside of the Laboratory, but then strange alien patterns swirl on the screen. They make you feel odd. You cannot pull your eyes away. You are falling asleep! Suddenly you hear a loud bleep. Something hard knocks your arm. The data pad falls to the ground and you blink awake. That was close! What saved you?

Vineeta is the chief scientist, but she is not the station commander. Check the table again.

Go to page 29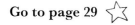

You study all the data you have collected, but you can't see a way to reverse all the damage done by the alien craft!

There is only one thing to do. You must go to the Communications dome to make contact with the aliens who built the recycling ships!

Go to page 14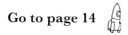

Zapie explains what he will do. If you can tell him how many microbots the unit has released, and provide him with the serial numbers of the worms, he will send the codes to reverse their recycling programs.

Luckily you have all the data on your data pad. You upload the information and observe what happens around the base on the video monitors.

Go to page 24

In the Habitat the microbots start to rebuild the damage. In the Biodome the plant spacecraft starts to shrink. The worms release nutrients back into the soil. Normal plants begin to grow again. In the Laboratory the alarms stop and the computers return to normal. Even the giant alien machine rebuilds the satellite dish it destroyed. The microbots, worms and data collection cables return to the tiny spacecraft in which they came. They will return to Planet Zorgon to be repaired.

Zapie apologizes again and comes up with a surprise.

"To make up for the trouble, we would like to invite you for a free holiday to Pirate Planet – the greatest theme park in the Universe!"

You cannot wait. You make sure there will be a place for Rhombus on the trip, too. He deserves it!

THE END

25

Your data pad has a camera – it can work as a powerful microscope. You hold the lens over one of the damaged spoons. This is what you see...

It looks as if the metal is being eaten by a swarm of tiny insects. You focus on one of the 'insects' and zoom to greater magnification. It's not an insect at all, it's a tiny alien machine, like a toy! It is cutting off pieces of metal and adding them to its body. As you watch, the alien machine grows before your eyes.

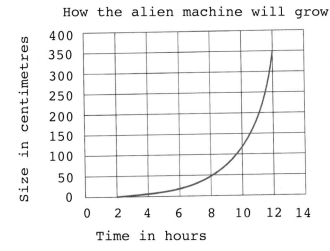

You program the data pad to plot a line graph to show how the alien will grow as it feeds. The data pad asks you to enter the size of the alien in 12 hours.

How the alien machine will grow

If you enter 3.5 cm, go to page 41 ☾ **If you enter 3.5 m, go to page 41** ☆

No – that's not correct! One of the giant bees leaves a tomato flower. It is heading straight for you! Its buzz is deafening. Its sting is as big as a dagger!

Then there is a loud beeping sound, like a warning. A cloud of smoke puffs over your shoulder at the bee. It flies away. That was close!

The tomato turns yellow after 6.5 seconds. It is fully ripe after 12.0 seconds. So the number of seconds it takes to turn from yellow to red is 12.0 – 6.5 seconds.

Go to page 39

You strike lucky! At the moment you enter 36, the arrows are pointing at 3 and 6. It was wise to choose the outcome with the greatest probability (chance)!

Go to page 42

You cross the launch pad and make your way to the Laboratory dome. Its airlock is still closed. There will be air inside!

Then you see a tiny alien craft. It has crash-landed next to the Laboratory entrance!

Your data pad translates the alien symbols on the craft's side as 'DATA GATHERING UNIT'. Black cables are snaking out of the unit. They are growing like ivy in every direction. One cable has reached the Laboratory. It has plugged itself into the data terminal on the airlock door!

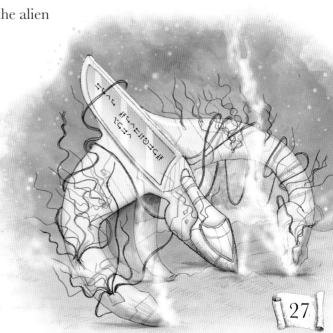

Go to page 12

There are far more damaged knives than spoons. Some things aren't damaged at all. It's a real puzzle! You organize the data in Carroll diagrams. You sort the items by colour; by size; by material. Here are two of the sorting tables you see on your data pad screen.

	Small	Big
Damaged	knives cans metal spoons metal cups	tables and chairs
Not damaged	plastic spoons plastic cups	computer screens windows

	Made from metal	Not made from metal
Damaged	tables and chairs knives drinks cans metal spoons metal cups	
Not damaged		plastic cups computer screens windows plastic spoons

You think you can see what links the damaged items! Your data pad asks you to tick the factor that all the damaged items have in common:

Small ☐   **Big** ☐   **Metal** ☐   **Non-metal** ☐

If you tick **Big**, go to page 7 ⚛   If you tick **Metal**, go to page 16 🪐

 Yes. Planet Z's atmosphere is more similar to Earth's. Could it be Planet Zorgon? You must send a signal and wait for a reply!

Go to page 5 ☆

You step down from your spaceship. The Habitat airlocks are wide open. This is where the crew eat, sleep and relax. Now it is empty, cold and airless. You look at the display on your data pad. It shows a table of the Alpha Base crew. You can call their mobile data pads by clicking the call signs next to their names. You try to contact the station commander.

Alpha Base crew

	Name	Age	Job
call	Greg	28	Communications
call	Vineeta	39	Chief scientist
call	Joe	27	Biologist
call	Amy	41	Station commander
call	Malav	45	Pilot and engineer
call	Sue	31	Doctor and scientist

If you click the call sign next to Vineeta, go to page 23

If you click the call sign next to Vineeta, go to page 23

If you click the call sign next to Amy, go to page 32

It's the wrong code! When you enter the 6 the first arrow is pointing to 3. The arrows spin faster. One of the cables from the alien craft starts to snake towards you. It's going to connect to your suit!

Then, with a loud beeping noise, a mechanical arm fitted with wire cutters reaches over your shoulder. The cutters snip through the cable. That was close!

There are three 3s on the first spinner, but only two 6s and one 4. This means that 3 has the highest chance of being the first digit. Which number has the highest chance of being the second digit?

Go to page 37

29

Your data pad plots the data in the frequency table as a bar chart.

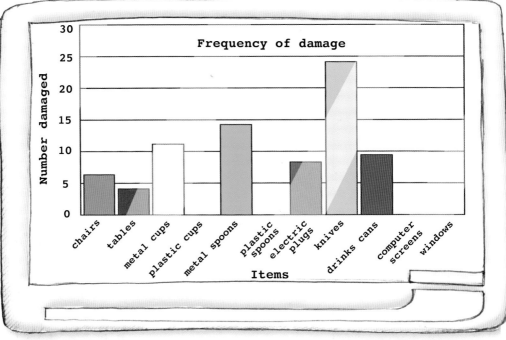

Frequency of damage

Why are some items damaged but not others? You try to make sense of the data. You compare numbers. How many more knives are damaged than metal spoons?

If you think 10 more knives are damaged, go to page 15

If you think 8 more knives are damaged, go to page 34

You've chosen the wrong combination! The airlock begins to fill with purple gas. It's starting to eat through your spacesuit! Then a jet of water sprays over your suit – where did that come from? The gas dissolves and washes away.

There are four possible colour combinations for the lights. In three of the four there is at least one green light. The chance of at least one green light is $\frac{3}{4}$ or 75%. The chance of two reds is only $\frac{1}{4}$ or 25%! Quickly, re-enter your choice.

Go to page 42

You decide to analyse the soil and water in the Biodome. You must find out what is happening! First you take a sample of the water from the water sprays.

   You know that plant food is added to the water, but you are amazed when you see the pie charts on your data pad!

Normal biodome water

natural minerals
plant food

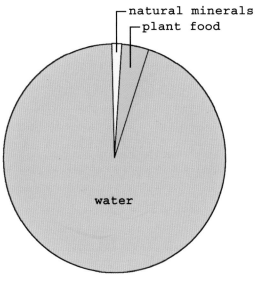

water

Contaminated water

natural minerals
plant food

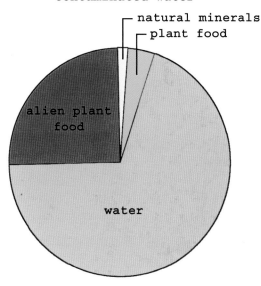

alien plant food

water

If you think the contaminated water contains 10% alien plant food, go to page 39

If you think the contaminated water contains 25% alien plant food, go to page 18

Oh no, it's an answerphone!

   "Thank you for calling Galactic Recycling Ltd. For sales enquiries please press 1. To track an existing order please press 2. For spares and servicing please press 3. For all other enquiries please hold."

   You hold.

Go to page 19

The temperature drops to −5°C. The worms stop moving. The alien craft stops growing. You have halted the recycling process!

But can the process be reversed? If not, the base's food and oxygen supply has been destroyed! You examine one of the recycling worms with your microscope.

The data pad translates the alien text on the worm's head as 'SERIAL NUMBER: X/002'. You store the number in your data pad.

Go to page 23

Your data pad puts through the call. Amy's pad returns a recorded message.

"Mayday! Mayday!" Amy's voice calls. "Something strange is happening. We are abandoning the Habitat to the aliens. We have left the data stick in a safe place. You will need it to save the station. My birthday is the key. But first you must find out what is causing the damage. Take care, the aliens may look like toys, but they grow! No more time…"

You do not understand all the message. But you decide to investigate – and to watch out for aliens that look like toys!

Go to page 8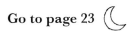

You connect the cable to the solar cells. Then, unwinding the cable as you go, you head back to the Habitat. You connect the other end of the cable to the metal frame. When the planet's two suns rise, the electric current should stop the aliens in their tracks!

Go to page 9

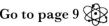

As you enter 1100, a warning message appears:

CAUTION: SERIOUS DATA ERROR

That's too few! If you get the number wrong, some microbots may still be active! The key shows that you should count in thousands as you point at the whole pictograms. Don't forget to add the two half pictograms – they stand for 500 each.

Go to page 21 ☆

You explain your discoveries to the crew. No one has heard of Planet Zorgon! Together you decide to use the base telescope to search nearby star systems for likely planets. The computer analyses the telescope data from the ten nearest star systems.

Ten nearest star systems	
	Number of planets
Star system 1	3
Star system 2	6
Star system 3	8
Star system 4	5
Star system 5	8
Star system 6	5
Star system 7	11
Star system 8	8
Star system 9	2
Star system 10	8

You talk about the data. When you say the number which is the mode for the number of planets, Rhombus beeps loudly!

If you think the mode is 11,

go to page 36 🪐

If you think the mode is 8,

go to page 8 🚀

No, that's not correct! The height of the columns shows the number of damaged knives is 24; the number of damaged spoons is 14. What is the difference between 24 and 14?

Go to page 30

You think the temperature is only 4.5°C. You turn up the heater inside your spacesuit. You operate the airlock and step into the Biodome.

It's like a sauna! Your helmet steams up. You are starting to pass out with the heat! Then something beeps loudly. A mechanical arm grabs you and pulls you back into the airlock. You start to cool down.

The thermometer scale runs from 0°C to 100°C. Each major division is 10 degrees.

Go to page 7 🌙

Another alien message appears on the Laboratory monitor. You use your translation program:

**DATA GATHERING HALTED
UNEXPECTEDLY**

**FOR TECHNICAL SUPPORT CALL
PLANET ZORGON 112 345 2011**

**STANDARD INTERPLANETARY CALL
CHARGES WILL APPLY
PLEASE CHECK YOUR SERVICE
PROVIDER FOR RATES**

You have never heard of Planet Zorgon, but you guess that is where the data gathering spacecraft came from! You make a note of the number. You decide you must try to make contact with this mysterious planet. Their tiny spacecraft must be stopped!

Go to page 14

The Habitat power is down. Your spacesuit does not have enough power to pass electricity through all the aliens. You must find a power source!

Then you remember the solar cells on the base plan. If you can connect them to the Habitat dome, that should do the trick!

You click back to the plan on your data pad. This time you overlay a grid to help you plan your route.

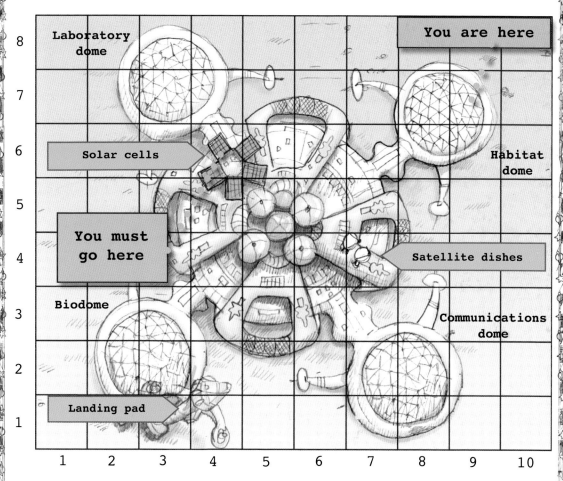

You are in grid square 9, 7. You must program your data pad to guide you to the solar panels.

If you enter your destination as 4, 6 go to page 4

If you enter your destination as 6, 4 go to page 18

You upload the Skaro virus onto the Laboratory computers. It's the wrong one! Now there are two viruses on the system. The chaos in the Laboratory gets worse! The reactor starts to vibrate and smoke!

Look again at the patterns. You could hold page 20 to the mirror to see what their mirror images look like.

Quickly you make copies of the Skaro virus on your data pad. You flip them horizontally and vertically to make mirror images. Then you upload the mirror images to the Laboratory computers. It works. The virus patterns are cancelled! The reactor stops vibrating so wildly.

Go to page 20

You enter the word 'SHIP' on the data pad. It starts to vibrate. Laser beams flash in all directions from its screen. It could explode!

You got the translation wrong! Look at the symbols in the table. Which letter comes below the first symbol ⅄? Quickly – try the translation again.

Go to page 9

Rhombus gets agitated. His head spins and he jumps up and down! It's the wrong number!

The mode is the most frequent (common) value in a set of data. Quickly, choose another number before Rhombus blows a fuse!

Go to page 33

You request the entry code from your data pad. It should be a two-digit number like 66. But instead of two digits, the display shows two spinners. The arrows spin wildly as a virus changes the digits at random...

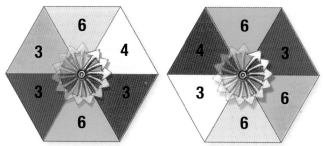

Which number should you enter? You decide your best chance is to enter the most probable digit from each spinner

If you enter 63, go to page 29   **If you enter 36, go to page 27**

That's the wrong direction! Rhombus tries to put the piece in place but it does not fit! The alien is starting to recover from the shock. His mechanical hand starts to snip at the metal. You must hurry! Give Rhombus the correct instruction.

Look again at the shape. You must turn it to the right ↷ to make it fit the gap.

Go to page 5

You upload the Kronos virus to the Laboratory computers. You made the right choice. The Kronos virus patterns cancel out their mirror images. Through the dome view port you see the data cable from the alien craft start to smoke. Then it disconnects from the airlock terminal. It snakes back into the alien craft. It did not like the effects of your 'anti-virus'!

The computers reboot. Things start to operate normally again. But not the reactor. It starts to glow with blue radiation. It is out of control!

Go to page 15

It's the wrong number! As you start to write 12, a message flashes on the screen... 'SYSTEM ERROR – SHUTTING DOWN'. Oh no! Without your data pad you will be helpless!

A tally is a way to record numbers of things or events. The table that shows the numbers is a frequency table. In this frequency table each tally mark stands for 1.

Quickly, check the spoon tally again!

Go to page 8

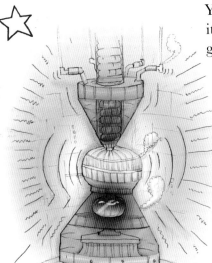

You cut the reactor power supply. But it has no effect. The radiation glow gets brighter!

A probability of 1 is certainty. A probability of 0.5 means that something is equally likely to happen or to not happen – like tossing heads with a fair coin. So there is still an even chance that the reactor will explode!

You should have chosen the action with the lowest probability of producing an explosion. There is still just time to make another choice!

Go to page 15

You press the airlock entry button. A message on the entry display says 'Secure area. Enter base security codes'.

You enter the codes downloaded from the data stick. The airlock operates. As you enter the airlock, you realize that something is coming in with you! It's Rhombus, the Alpha Base maintenance robot. He has been helping you all along!

Go to page 41

You watch as a giant tomato falls from a plant to the ground. In seconds it rots to mush on the soil. The seeds start to sprout. New tomato plants grow before your eyes. They flower. Huge bees buzz around. The flowers become fruits and new tomatoes ripen.

You use your data pad to record a video of a tomato fruit growing. This is what you see when you play the video back:

| 0.0 seconds | 2.0 seconds | 4.5 seconds | 6.5 seconds | 8.0 seconds | 12.0 seconds |

How many seconds does it take the tomato to ripen from yellow to red?

If you think it takes 12.0 seconds, go to page 27

If you think it takes 5.5 seconds, go to page 5

No, there is much more alien food in the water than that!

Suddenly the strength of the water spray rises. It is so strong it knocks you to the ground. Then a mechanical foot stands on the main hose and blocks the water supply.

The 'slices' in a pie chart show the fractions of the different parts that make up the whole pie. The 'alien plant food' slice of the Biodome water is a quarter of the whole. What is one quarter as a percentage?

Go to page 31

As you watch the aliens on a copper wire, they all run to one end. They are pushing the wire towards you like a needle – it's going to puncture your spacesuit!

Suddenly a mechanical arm reaches over your shoulder. There is a loud beep followed by a blue flash. A bolt of electricity runs down the wire. The aliens freeze as the electricity passes through their bodies.

That's it! Electricity! All metals conduct electricity! Somehow you must pass an electric current through all the metal objects in the Habitat. That will stop the aliens!

Go to page 35

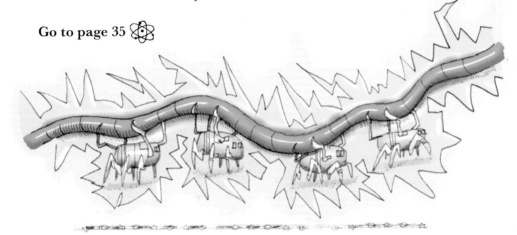

 You decide to examine the soil to see why it has fewer worms. You reach down and pick up a handful. You were wrong. It is full of wriggling, writhing worms!

But these are not ordinary worms! They have slimy worm bodies, but their heads are mechanical, with sharp chomping teeth! They start to chomp at your glove. You shake your hand, but they do not let go!

Look at the size of the worm fraction in the Biodome soil bar on the chart. It is much bigger than in normal soil.

Just as the worms are about to chew through your glove a mechanical arm reaches over your shoulder. It sprays the worms with a freezing cold liquid. They stop wriggling and drop to the ground. That was close! Someone is looking out for you!

Go to page 10

That's correct! In just 12 hours the alien machine will be 3.5 metres tall. That's as tall as a lamp post! Just think how much damage it will do then! And there must be thousands of them loose in the Habitat. You must act quickly!

Go to page 17

As you enter 3.5 cm, the aliens turn and look into the camera lens. The alien swarm gathers on the spoon and starts to march. They are marching towards you! If they get onto your spacesuit they will eat all the metal parts!

Then behind you there is a loud beeping. A plastic cup bangs down over the spoon – trapping the aliens inside. That was close! Who or what did that?

The graph shows that in 12 hours' time the alien will be 350 cm tall! How many metres is that?

Go to page 26

The inner airlock door opens. You and Rhombus step inside the Communications dome. You are greeted by a loud cheer! This is where the crew have taken shelter. They are all here!

Station commander Amy explains how they observed a shooting star. Then they lost control of the base systems. All the crew gathered in the only high security part of Alpha Base – the Communications dome.

They managed to send an SOS message, but then the Communications computers crashed. They have been infected by the same virus as the Laboratory computers!

You know how to cure that! You upload the Kronos virus to the computers. Instantly they reboot. Now you can try to contact the aliens!

Go to page 33

The outer door of the airlock slides open. You step through. The outer door closes. Inside you press the button marked OPERATE. But nothing happens! The airlock should fill with air so you can take off your helmet. Then the inner door should open.

You are trapped inside!

You see the two airlock safety lights are flashing randomly red and green. A virus has made the controls crash. You see four colour combinations...

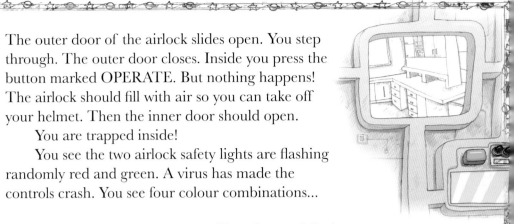

RED RED   **RED GREEN**

GREEN RED   **GREEN GREEN**

Your data pad flashes a message...

```
Click on the more likely
combination to make the door
operate.
Take care, the wrong choice will
cause a dangerous breakdown!
```

At least one green light, go to page 14 ☆

Two red lights, go to page 30 🪐

You made the correct choice. Restarting the reactor computer is the best action to choose. It gives the lowest probability of an explosion.

If a probability is 1 then something is certain to happen. If it is 0 then it will definitely not happen. A probability of 0.1 means that there is a probability of only one out of ten (10%) that the event will happen. Nine times out of ten the reactor will not explode.

As the computer restarts it regains control of the reactor. The reactor cools and the radiation glow disappears. The countdown stops at 0.3 seconds – just in time!

Go to page 34 ☆

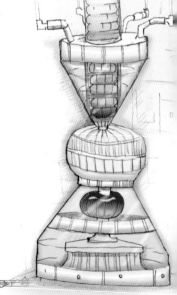

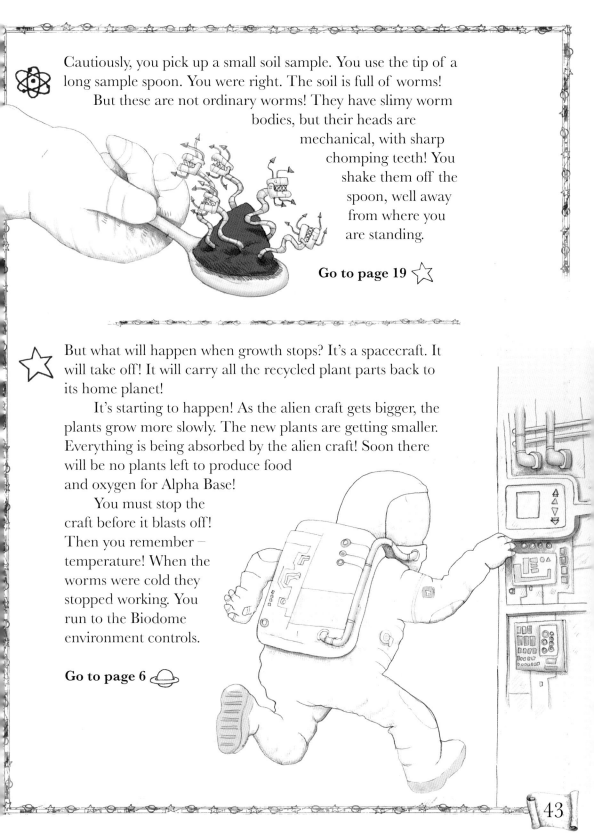

Cautiously, you pick up a small soil sample. You use the tip of a long sample spoon. You were right. The soil is full of worms!

But these are not ordinary worms! They have slimy worm bodies, but their heads are mechanical, with sharp chomping teeth! You shake them off the spoon, well away from where you are standing.

Go to page 19 ☆

But what will happen when growth stops? It's a spacecraft. It will take off! It will carry all the recycled plant parts back to its home planet!

It's starting to happen! As the alien craft gets bigger, the plants grow more slowly. The new plants are getting smaller. Everything is being absorbed by the alien craft! Soon there will be no plants left to produce food and oxygen for Alpha Base!

You must stop the craft before it blasts off! Then you remember – temperature! When the worms were cold they stopped working. You run to the Biodome environment controls.

Go to page 6 🪐

bar chart

A bar chart uses bars to display data. The heights of the bars compare the sizes or numbers of different things.

On this bar chart the bars show the amounts of different gases present in the atmosphere.

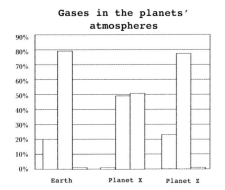

Gases in the planets' atmospheres

On this bar chart the bars are divided up to show the percentages of different components that make up soil.

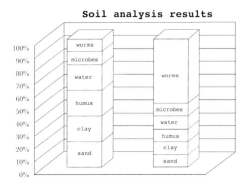

Soil analysis results

Carroll diagram

A Carroll diagram is a way of sorting things into sets that do and do not have one or more properties. Carroll diagrams were invented by mathematician Charles Dodgson who also called himself Lewis Carroll. He is the author of *Alice's Adventures in Wonderland*.

In this Carroll diagram objects are sorted into four sets: damaged and metal; damaged and not metal; not damaged and metal; not damaged and not metal.

	Made from metal	Not made from metal
Damaged	tables and chairs knives drinks cans metal spoons metal cups	
Not damaged		computer screens windows plastic spoons

coordinates

Coordinates are numbers or letters that give the position of a point on a graph, a grid or a map. The first number or letter gives the position along the horizontal axis. The second number or letter gives the position along the vertical axis.

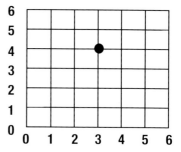

The coordinates of the point marked on this grid are 3, 4.

data

Data are numbers and/or words that you measure or record. They are a form of information. The information and facts stored on a computer are called computer data.

flow chart

A flow chart is a diagram that shows the steps in a process or the solution to a problem. You could draw a flow chart to describe how to tie a shoelace or how to do long division, for example.

frequency table

A frequency table records the numbers of events or things in a certain time or place. This is called their 'frequency'. You could use a frequency table to record the numbers of birds of different species seen in a day in your garden.

line graph

A line graph is a diagram that shows how one thing changes as another changes (the height of a plant as time passes, for example). The scales for the two things compared are shown along the horizontal and vertical axes of the graph. This graph shows how the height of an alien (vertical axis) increases with time (horizontal axis).

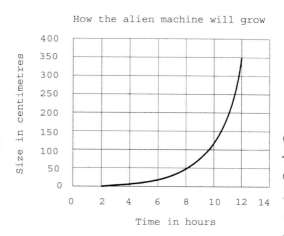

mean, median and mode

The mean, median and mode are different properties of a set of numbers (the ages of the children in a school, for example). The mean is the average: you could find this by adding all the ages together and dividing by the number of children. The median is the middle value in the set: if you write all the ages in order from lowest to highest, the median is the age half way down the list. The mode is the most common value in the set: if there are more eight-year-olds than any other age, then eight is the mode.

pictogram

A pictogram uses pictures or symbols instead of words or numbers to show information.

This pictogram shows the numbers of alien microbots in the alien spacecraft.

SPECIFICATION:

IRON AND STEEL MICROBOTS

COPPER MICROBOTS

ALUMINIUM MICROBOTS

GOLD MICROBOTS

Key	
	= 1000
	= 500

pie chart

A pie chart shows how something is shared out or divided up. The whole is drawn as a circle, which is divided into parts like the slices of a pie. The size of a slice tells you the fraction of the whole made up from that part. This pie chart shows that one quarter of the contaminated water is alien plant food.

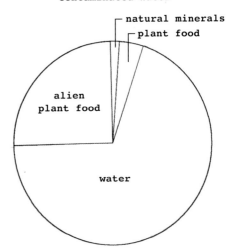

Contaminated water

natural minerals
plant food

alien plant food

water

probability

Probability is the mathematical word for chance. If something is certain to happen its probability is 1 or 100%. If it is equally likely to happen or not happen (for example tossing heads with a fair coin) the probability is ½ or 50%. If something is certain not to happen the probability is 0.

range

The range of a set of numbers or data is the difference between the lowest value and the highest value.

table

A table is a chart displaying data in rows and columns. It could show measurements from an experiment, scores in a game or prices for items in a shop. Almost any kind of data can be organized into table form.

tally

A tally is an easy way to record the numbers of different things or events. Each thing is recorded with a mark. To make it simpler to count up the final total, the fifth mark is made through the previous four; ⅡⅡ stands for 5, the line through the first four marks counts as a mark, too.

Venn diagram

A Venn diagram is one way to organize things into sets. The sets are shown by circles. Each thing is put inside the sets to which it belongs. In a Venn diagram the sets can overlap. In the diagram below iron belongs to both the set of materials that are metals and the set of materials that are magnetic.

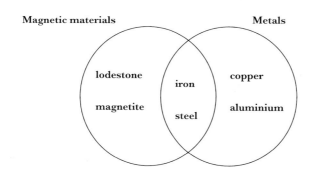

Notes for parents and teachers

The Maths Quest series of books is designed to motivate children to develop and apply their maths skills through engaging adventure stories. The stories work as games in which the children must solve a series of mathematical problems to make progress towards the exciting conclusion.

The books do not follow a conventional pattern. The reader is directed to jump forwards and back through the book according to the answers they give to the problems. If their answers are correct, they make progress to the next part of the story; if they are incorrect the mathematics is explained, before the reader is directed back to try the problem again. Additional support may be found in the glossary at the back of the book.

To support your child's mathematical development you can:

• Read the book with your child.

• Solve the initial problems and discover how the book works.

• Continue reading with your child until he or she is using the book confidently, following the **Go to** instructions to find the next puzzle or explanation.

• Encourage your child to read on alone. Ask "What's happening now?" Prompt your child to tell you how the story develops and what problems they have solved.

• Discuss numbers in everyday contexts: shopping, filling up the car at the garage; looking at the car mileage and road signs when on journeys; using timetables; following recipes and so on.

• Have fun making up number sequences and patterns. Count in 2s, 3s, 4s and 5s and larger steps. Ask times-table questions to pass the time on journeys. Count backwards in different steps. List doubles, halves, square numbers and primes. Play "I'm thinking of a number, can you guess it?" games in which you ask questions such as "Is it even or odd?", "Is it bigger than 100?", "How many digits does it have?" and so on.

• Play number-based computer games with your child. These will hold children's interest with colourful graphics and lively animations as they practise basic number skills.

• Most of all, make maths fun!